AT LEAST THE DUCK SURVIVED

AT LEAST THE DUCK SURVIVED

Poems by Margaret Clough

modjaji books

Publication © Modjaji Books 2011
Text © Margaret Clough 2011

First published in 2011 by Modjaji Books Pty Ltd
P O Box 385, Athlone, 7760, South Africa
modjaji.books@gmail.com
http://modjaji.book.co.za
www.modjajibooks.co.za

ISBN: 978-1-920397-85-2

Book design: Natascha Mostert
Cover artwork and lettering: Danielle Clough
Author's photograph: Kerry Hammerton

Printed and bound by Mega Digital
Set in Palatino

Several of these poems were originally published in
Difficult to Explain, edited by Finuala Dowling and *Carapace.*

Contents

By Sandvlei Shore

Because I now have time
to sit and stare
at waving reeds and gently flowing water,
I am becoming like the river as it nears its end.
After its headlong rush
down granite cliffs,
and its busy journey through
the vineyards, and the fields,
arriving at
a wide and sandy beach, it's forced
to slow its pace,
to spread a little, to drop
its load of silty litter,
and to let
the ripples on its surface smooth away
so it can hold
reflections of the slow clouds
floating by.

Degrees of Separation

(in the exercise hall)

As my hands sway slowly to the music
and my feet are placed
in just the right angle to each other by the Tai Chi teacher
I can believe that I
am only a very few degrees of separation
from some old woman in Beijing
doing exercises in the park.

Moving On

So many homes
so much uprooting
so much of life spent relocating
clearing out, packing up and throwing things away
each move becoming a rehearsal
for the one last and final
removal.

Last Will and Testament

I want:
someone to have this bed
and lie awake at night listening
to the roar of surf
and the whine of the wind
and make up stories about them
for her grandchildren

I would like:
someone to drive this car
on rough roads on the mountain
and sandy tracks by the sea
and let children smear sticky fingers on the dashboard
and dogs shed hair on the seats

And I need:
someone to take this chair
with its fading upholstery and
the stuffing coming out at its seams
and fall asleep in it
watching the news
on the television.

It's Difficult to Explain

Why was my car standing as though abandoned in Waterford
road, you ask?
It is difficult to explain; it's a long story –
because my grandson drove it home,
because he took it to his work,
because it had to be repaired,
because it had a nasty dent,
because I ran into the gate,
because the gate began to close,
because its motor didn't work,
because the remote control was bust,
because it got wet in my jeans,
because I fell into a pond,
because I tried to catch the dog,
because she tried to catch a duck.
(At least the duck survived.)

Blind Maltese Poodle, Nutmeg

Brave little milk-eyed fluff bundle,
with Amazon heart and
Robert Bruce resolve.
See how she holds her head up high,
and waves her tail aloft.
Watch how she feels her way
over a wooden bridge.
A slip, a splash
then muddy, but unbowed,
she shakes herself and
goes across once more,
only to tumble off again
but on the other side.
Look how daintily she dances on the sand
happy to smell the sea and hear the waves.
When bothered by a barking boerbull,
note how she chases him down the beach
spectacular in her show of
snarling rage.

Telltales

I could tell a storm was coming
by the harshness of the seagull's cry
and the way the dog shivered
as he hid behind the chair
and the sound of the door, banging
and by seeing, lying at the sky's corners,
the fine-drawn strings of cloud
like the frown lines forming
round my eyes.

Epitaph

For Gertie

To look at, one might have said she was
a cross between a mole rat and a doormat,
perhaps a Cairn or Scottie in the line.
Lucky, when young, to have survived at all –
the others in the litter died.
A little shadow lost behind my skirt,
an undemanding presence in our home,
never too good at playing catch
or learning show-off tricks for visitors,
but grateful for a tidbit or a pat
or a short outing to the park.
Just
a little black dog.

Reunion at the Tearoom

The last time we were here there were five of us.
Five old girls playing at being wild,
letting our gray hair down,
wiping the tears of laughter from our eyes,
shouting each other down with bawdy reminiscence,
disgraceful and rowdy, seventeen again and tasting
immortality.

Today we sit here, you and I, with nothing left to say.
Our tea gets cold. Our scones lie on our plates.
Our fingers tremble, joints are stiff with pain.
Dry-eyed we hold each other's gaze.
We do not want to look to left or right
and see the empty chairs.

Luck

Luck is a lady
with a questionable taste in clothes
accessorising with mouldy
rabbits' feet
and smelly crows' feathers.
She has a weakness for
coats put on inside out
and vests worn back to front.
But with this lack of care
in her attire,
she is very fussy about
spilt salt, cracked mirrors
and the way the wind blows.
She sits on my veranda
with a mangy black cat on her lap,
watching me out of one squinting beady eye,
making sure
that I don't step on cracks in the patio pavement
or start anything new
on a Friday.

Failing Memory

The years squeeze up and squash into each other
I travel on a backward-moving train
into a once-familiar country,
but through the window I can only see
glimpses of trees and houses and of fields
and sometimes people filling out the scenes.
Here's an old woman baking bread
and a young one picking apples;
there I see children playing catch,
a man walking a dog.
That woman with her hair tied up in plaits,
holding a toddler by the hand:
I think I know her, but I can't be sure.
That boy with hazel eyes
didn't I once fall in love with him?
– Or was it someone else?
The train moves faster on its shining rails
leaving them all behind.

Unscheduled

I would rather not
go on this journey
tourist class
feet dangling,
hand luggage entangled in
chair arm's electronics.
I want a proper passport into
a different life,
but
I am suspended
(empty space around me)
trying to forget about
crashes and disasters,
closing ears to
engine wail,
trying to ignore the turbulence
of duties not performed.
Strings of life
are tangled.
Straps and buckles are too tight.
Scraps sticking to my hands
and threads hanging on my clothing,
I am borne away,
trailing miscellaneous clobber
into a new dimension.

Faith

Not the stained glass window warrior
sword in hand,
nor the sea captain, steadfast through the storm,
but warmth spreading slowly under thick blankets,
and in the darkness
remembering the feel
of a small hand closing round my finger.
Outside my window
a sudden owl swoops then flies back
to make a quiet moaning in the pines.
I hear the rustle of birds.
Dawn coming.
I am aware of wings.

Serenity

Steam rises from a teapot on the table,
reflected on its rounded metal belly are
the painted flowers on the milk jug
and the china cups, which stand
snug in their saucers, ready to be filled.
A cat curls on the sofa, silky fur
striped grey and white,
licked smooth and clean.
The floor shines wetly and
the tumblers washed and dried line up
in tidy rows on a high shelf.
A broken glass lies safe inside the bin.
Bottles are stoppered and the cupboard closed.

If I Come Back Again

If I come back again
will it be
to look over your shoulder?
What are you reading now?
Something we used to share
or a new novel, one I do not know?
Will you hear my footsteps sometimes
creaking through the house or
my fingers tapping on the keys?
Will you still keep bits of me:
the pens I constantly mislaid,
the broken spectacles abandoned on the shelf,
the chipped cup I always meant
to throw away?
Will it be like a ripple
on a puddle after rain,
a shadow falling
on the paving by the gate,
or perhaps
like a needle slipping in the hand,
just for a moment,
sharp and
piercing?

Against Symphony Concerts

You have to be so careful not to cough
or let your programme rustle.
However moved you are, you mustn't wave your arms
or ululate in that rude township way, and please
remember not to clap between the movements.
However much you hate Shostakovich
you must endure him first before
the orchestra will let you hear some Bach.
Does anybody really like
solos for bassoon or double bass,
even when played by visiting celebrities?
Isn't it much nicer here at home
where we can loll on easy chairs
sip Merlot and enjoy our own CDs?

If Someone Came Now Offering Love

How delighted I would be.
It would be so exciting,
so unexpected:
a lottery win on a forgotten ticket, or
a legacy from a long lost cousin.
But:–
I would have nowhere to put it.
If I sat it on my garden bench
it would get spoilt in the rain.
I could find place for it in the front window,
but the residents' aesthetics committee might object.
The kitchen cupboards are too full of pots and pans,
tins of baked beans, spaghetti and dog biscuits
and the computer fills up all the space in the study.
And as for the bedroom –
No. I wouldn't want it there.
I think I would have to wrap it carefully in sacking,
stitch it up with a large curved needle
and mark it with a thick black pen
"Return to sender."

What Are You Doing This Evening?

What am I doing this evening?
Don't know – it just depends –
So if –
you want to fly me to a tropic isle
to walk at sunset with you on the beach,
dig bare toes into the wet soft sand
and watch the moon rise bright behind the palms
or if –
you have a special restaurant in mind,
where you can treat me to a feast
of lobster, sole and oysters, fillet steak
all followed by a sweet of *crème brûlée*
or if –
you have bought tickets to "La Boheme"
with Sibongele in the lead and we
can feed our souls with sound and afterwards
you've hired a limousine to drive us home.
Why then –
I've nothing planned; I'm quite
at your disposal.

But if – as I suspect –
you have a pile of washing; your machine
has broken down and cannot be repaired, your shirt
has lost its buttons and your cat
needs taking to the vet.
Why then, my love,
I might say I am otherwise engaged, but yet
I've not the heart – I'm really quite
at your disposal still.

Robyn at the School Gates

I sit and shiver at the steering wheel
harassed by hooting and by thunder.
Lightning crackles on the radio
and windscreen wipers fight the rain.
In the snarled traffic, cars shine wet and headlamps
silver the swirls of water on the road.
As you splash sodden to the car, you smile:
– Isn't it beautiful? you say.

After the Rain

After the rain,
hot sun on a steaming road
and in a puddle,
    flash of red,
    spatter of silver,
    wriggle of joy,
a starling takes a bath.

To Isabel

Here it is almost night and the west wind
is blowing blobs of rain against my door;
my fingers stiffen and my feet get cold, but
where you are sitting colouring a picture,
of yellow sunflowers to send to me
the sky is cloudless and
the sun is rising.

To a Daughter

I walked on the mountain today among the spiky yellow
conebushes.
White knobs of Berzelia brushed me on either side.
The air was thick with the smell of buchu and of honey.
The wind was strong up there: seventy kilometres an hour or
more.
It blew my dog's ears back against her head.
I fought it all the way up to the peak before it knocked me over.
Walking home among the other old climbers
with weary legs and aching feet
I was as proud as if I'd conquered Everest.
I had just heard that I was to be a great-grandmother.
I never expected that I'd live so long.
I remember the day you were born;
it doesn't seem long ago to me.
It was Christmas time and a choir was singing carols
when I took you in my arms for the first time

Christmas

I remember
a pile of presents
and the embarrassment –
not knowing which to open first,
the only child and all the adults
sitting around me, watching
and then, the paper hats and the goose,
and finding a tickey in the pudding:
all too much for one day.
It ended in tears and being carried to bed
kicking and sobbing.

My daughters remember
singing carols round the piano,
stealing a Christmas tree
from the empty lot next door,
midnight mass and gathering mistletoe;
turkey and plum pudding and brandy butter,
guests squashed in around the table,
and silly parlour games.

My granddaughter remembers
coming to the Christmas house,
jumping out of the car to be the first to greet us
and, one Christmas eve,
seeing an angel standing on the stairs.

The First Southeaster of the Year

The south east wind
after a damp and doleful absence,
came back triumphant
rowdy and roaring,
keeping me from sleep,
tearing the soft green buds from off the trees,
chasing the sheepish clouds across the bay,
overturning boats and bicycles.
It pushed against us up the hill
as we went on our mountain ramble.
It tried to force us to turn back;
it nearly beat us, but we won;
we made it to the peak,
sat on the sheltered side,
ate sandwiches and listened to
the wind's frustrated howling.

Cape Weeds

On either side the road,
gray, spray-painted squalor,
pockmarked poverty.
Sodden faces stare
through jagged glass.
Men line the road-side,
dull-eyed and jobless
by dirt-dark puddles

Then suddenly –
Spring holidays, streets surge
with young and happy faces,
eager as the small tough daisies
that spring up everywhere,
between the plastic bags and broken bottles
carpeting the dusty empty spaces
with their round centres and bright yellow rays
children's drawings of the sun

Phone Calls

When the telephone rang at dawn
I knew it was my daughter, Dot
wanting an advance on her allowance.
"Just fifty rand – I'll pay you back" –
she never did.

I would complain,
grumble at having to get up early,
shout, angry, down the line
"This is the very last time"–
it never was.

In the early morning
I wake up to the sound of doves.
Still half asleep I listen for
the telephone to ring, but now –
it never does.

Emigration of my Daughter

I thought that it could last forever.
I thought that I would always be
wrapped in a comfort-blanket,
spoon-fed, cosseted,
with you at hand
ready to rock me,
soothe fretful cries and wipe away the tears,
that you'd still bring me pretty things to hold
and let the children pet and play with me.
But now you take your hand away from mine,
pry loose my fingers,
set me on my feet,
push me to shaky steps away from you.
You have been too long spoiling me, my child.
The time has come
to undertake a weaning.

Early Years

No poet should possess a past like mine —
a childhood bland as lemonade.
No shameful secret out of which to shape a sonnet,
no hurt or harm to turn into an ode,
just long and lazy days under the orchard trees
telling myself stories.

Born, shoe-box sized, focus of parents' dotage,
in Transvaal suburb. Then in the Cape
my life expanded
into large house, packed with a thousand books,
garden and orchard, trees for climbing, hedges to hide in
and family too extended,
to cousins, grandparents and aunts —
particularly aunts.

My early years were thronged with lady lesbians,
tweed-skirted kindly couples,
shingle-haired and Sappho-serious,
walking their dogs together every Sunday,
secure in their shared spinsterhood: but I,
lovesick, gazed with longing
on burly bearded men.
And later married one
who rescued me, romantic,
and bore me off to foreign parts,
like knight of old,
Lochinvar, but on a motorbike.

Bicycles

Whenever I think of bicycles
I see my mother,
small and bravely pedaling,
precariously perched,
handlebars held tight as though,
if given its head,
the thing might buck her off.
Each day she wobbled off
unsteadily to work,
flopped off triumphant, thankful
at the end of the completed journey.
And then stood
before her class of eager students,
strong and confident.

In the Laboratory

My Aunt Grace used to teach psychology
at a small university college.
In her laboratory on the third floor
she and I had fun together
with IQ tests and Rorschach blots.
Outside the window, an owl
watched us from the branch of a pine tree.
Along one side of the room
Jung, Freud and Skinner sat on shelves.
There was a model of the human brain in a cupboard.
You could take it apart:
cerebrum, cerebellum, medulla oblongata
and then fit it together,
matching the white and grey matter.
When the college closed,
the textbooks were packed in boxes
and the brain was sent off in pieces.
Then Aunt Grace died, but before that
the owl flew away.

To my Cousin Jerry

Do you remember – you said
– the time Aunt Enid fell in the river
and what a loud noise she made
and how on the way home her crimplene dress
went on shrinking and shrinking
right up her thighs to
above her suspenders,
and do you remember picking plums in the orchard,
red juice running down our chins
and the family teas
with cream cakes and scones and gossip
and Uncle Walter falling asleep in the middle.

We remember and remembering for a while forget
our nowadays of shaky hands and shuffling feet.

Mauve

My Aunt Maud's dress,
a melancholy mauve,
reflects the colour
of the evening sky
as she stoops to plant petunias
in the pots beside her door.
Her skirt rucks up,
her corset groans.
Her eyes are watering in the fading light.
Her chin quivers,
but her hands
cradle each seedling
as she tucks it in.

Remembering First Love

My longing like
an impacted tooth's persistent ache,
the dentist's drill grinds the cracked molar, but
shutting my eyes I feel his hand in mine.
The whirling metal whines,
but it's his voice
that murmurs in my ear.
At school the lessons
blur and merge together.
Equations, dates of battles,
continents and seas
have all become
the echo of his name.
He is at my fingertips,
scratched on my ruler and my pencil case.
My life is stuck fast
onto a telephone receiver
to be picked up
when he calls.

Touching Tribute to Shirley Valentine

("The right breast of a statue depicting Shirley Valentine has been worn thin by women rubbing it to bring them luck in love."
Cape Times 10 August 2010)

Fishermen pull boats up on the beach.
Fine hairs glisten on their muscled arms.
Dark eyes stare boldly.
Black sea-soaked curls dry salty
in the sun.
They spread out nets;
make ready for a catch.
From the shore,
she watches
spattered with seagull droppings,
worn out and wearied by
the desires of
fat northern females
looking for romance.

Worry

You believe in it;
like vitamins and green vegetables.
Collect it daily
with the bread and milk.
Carry it with you when out jogging
or at the beach.
(You never know when you might need it.)
It can also be used externally
to smear over other's pain and
you must never forget
to take a double dose on Sundays
on your knees, so God can worry too.

Nightmare

My mother
gave me a cat to hold
when she took me on a visit
to some people I didn't know.
The host's German shepherd
tried to bite it, but
got my sleeve in his mouth instead.
A Rottweiler backed him up.
We escaped to another room, where
there were Germans
shouting Sieg Heil and singing Horst Wessel.
When we left –
"Thank you very much for the lovely dinner" –
the door closed behind us.
My mother waved to me
and drove away in a little red car.
My handbag got left behind.
I went back to fetch it.
A strange girl opened the gate.
She took me round by a different door
and when she handed me my bag, I saw
she wasn't a girl after all,
but quite an old woman.
Back on the street, I couldn't find my car.
I walked up one road
and then another,
past a church – a funeral.
Mourners came out
carrying guns.
One of them spoke to me,
an ex-gangster I used to know.
My car was not in the car park
and the numbers on the bays had been changed

I tried to call my mother
to come and rescue me,
but where she'd gone
there was no network cover.
I didn't know how to get home
and I still had to go back
for the cat.

Puzzle of the Participle

I'm afraid I've quite forgotten
Whether to say got or gotten.
Was my jersey shrunk or shrunken?
Was the brandy drunk or drunken?
If the root of bought is buy
Can the verb from fraught be fruy?

Lexicography

Hobgoblins hugger-mugger
and hoity-toity as
they practise
hodge-podge hocus-pocus
for Hogmanay.

Day 0 + 8

(Nietzsche thought God would be bored after the seventh day.)

How could God have been bored
with all those new toys to play with?
Stars to toss about the sky,
comets to track across the constellations,
galaxies to rearrange.

And then he could watch Adam and Eve
exploring Eden,
discovering all the herbs and trees and bushes
just sprung from the ground
and giving them their names.

Wouldn't he delight in the words
they thought up:
Oleander and Love-in-a-mist,
Cotoneaster and Lily-of-the-valley,
Marjoram and Lavender.

But if he was in need of entertainment,
perhaps that's when, for fun,
he fitted swivel eyes to the Chameleon,
dressed the Penguin in a dinner jacket
and stuck that silly outsized beak
onto the Pelican.

Second Sight

All my myopic life,
when looking at the sky by night,
I've seen three moons.
When crescent they are folded
like the petals of an opening flower.
When full –
three pale orbs overlapping one another.
Now after surgery,
performed on one eye only,
I see two moons.
One is a pale and shiny blue,
the other one,
a murky yellow.
People tell me there is only one moon
and only one right way to view reality,
but I
know better.

Committal

Rain has pressed dust into the ground.
Ashes and mud lie there beneath our feet.
Carried on the cold air,
are graceless, gabbled sounds.
The empty urns are cracked.
A rash of lichen creeps across
the carved words on the stones.
Torn paper cups, brown petals and confetti
litter the pathway to the gate.
Behind the hedge where piles of leaves lie rotting
we can hear echoes of
the voices of children.

The Game

She was the one who thought it up:
it was the most popular game that term.
The children all came
to the churchyard garden.
They all wanted to have a turn,
to lie flat on the ground
and be covered all over
with fallen leaves,
while their friends laid wreaths of plaited grass,
sang hymns and wailed.
Only five of us are here for her today
bringing one sheaf of lilies and a bunch of roses.

Some games go out of fashion.

Afterword

After the petals have fallen from the wreaths
and the cards gone from the mantelpiece,
the letters written,
the clothes packed up,
the bills accounted for,
the plates the neighbours brought
sent back, washed clean,
then like a gray and greasy rat,
sliding out of a hole at dusk
comes ugly, sharp-toothed Sorrow.

Black Hole

Coming out of a black hole the other day
I met myself going in
and I wondered
what either of us could be doing there
in that place on the knife edge where
the past and future meet,
somewhere that isn't anywhere, but just
an emptiness that swallows up the light,
a heaviness that grows out of the night
amongst the shining beauty of the stars.
And as I peered out at the brim
I wondered how it possibly could be
that I, coming out, could meet me going in.

Other poetry titles by Modjaji Books

Fourth Child
by Megan Hall

Life in Translation
by Azila Talit Reisenberger

Burnt Offering
by Joan Metelerkamp

Oleander
by Fiona Zerbst

Strange Fruit
by Helen Moffett

Please, Take Photographs
by Sindiwe Magona

removing
by Melissa Butler

Missing
by Beverly Rycroft

These are the Lies I told you
by Kerry Hammerton

The Suitable Girl
by Michelle McGrane

Conduit
by Sarah Frost

www.modjajibooks.co.za